LOGBOOK
for little ships

Name of vessel: . . . .

Owner/Skipper: . . . .

Home Port: . . . .

Type/Class: . . . .

LOA.: . . . .   Draft: . . . .   Beam: . . . .

Call sign: . . . .

Sail Number:. Off. No./SSR no. . . . .

photo

CONTENTS

Log index

Date(s)	Voyage

INTRODUCTION

A log book can be more than a navigation aid, it can also be a complete sailing diary.

Most of our sailing consists of sociable summer weekends on familiar waters punctuated by occasional cruising holidays to new places. For navigation on longer passages we need hour by hour log keeping; for pottering we just need to note down times of high water and weather forecasts. We also like plenty of space for narrative, photographs and the odd menu/leaflet/thingy that we paste into the log. Once the season is over it is then much more enjoyable to look back on the whole story of our summer cruising.

We designed this log to be flexible enough for traditional navigation but also to allow space for a more complete narrative of where we went and who we met along the way.

Every sailor we spoke to has their favoured methods of log keeping, so we decided to leave the columns on the navigation side of the page blank to suit your own preferences and the type of sailing you do.

We hope our log book helps to make your cruising more enjoyable as well as seamanlike!

Claudia   *Perry*

Claudia Myatt and Perry Crickmere
Yacht 'Torhilda'

Notes on passage planning:

Under current SOLAS V (Safety of Life at Sea) regulations, all vessels that proceed to sea (including pleasure craft) must have in place an adequate passage plan. The level of detail necessary will depend on the type of boat, its crew and intended voyage. There are no specific requirements for pleasure vessels of less than 150 gt to keep a detailed log, although all pleasure craft are encouraged to maintain a log book as a matter of good practice. For further information on UK pleasure vessel regulations and recommendations, contact the RYA (www.rya.org.uk).

Date: . . . .

Crew: . . . .

. . . .

From: . . . .   Towards: . . . .

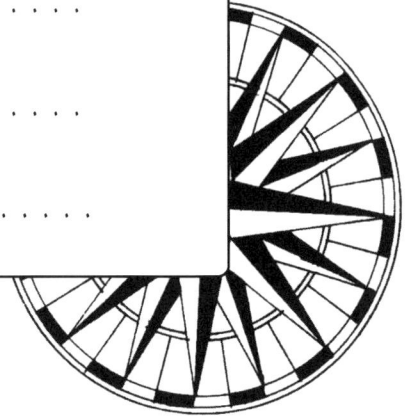

Passage Notes

HW

LW

TIME					

Date: . . . .

Crew: . . . .

. . . .

From: . . . .   Towards: . . . .

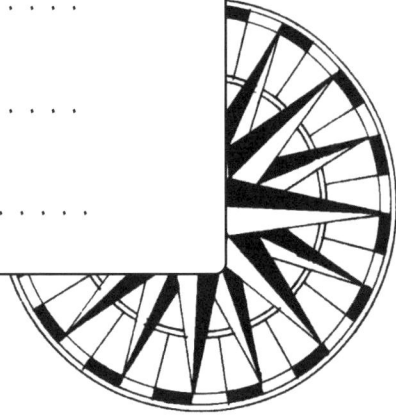

Passage Notes

HW

LW

TIME					

Date: . . . .

Crew: . . . .

. . . .

From: . . . . Towards: . . . .

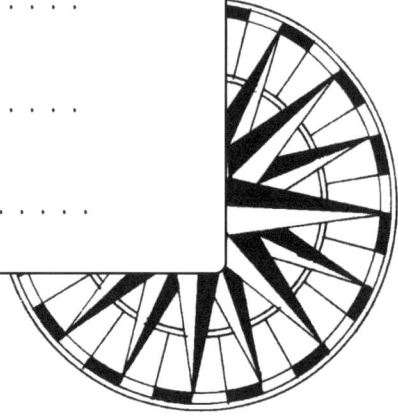

Passage Notes

HW

LW

TIME					

Date: . . . .

Crew: . . . .

. . . .

From: . . . .   Towards: . . . .

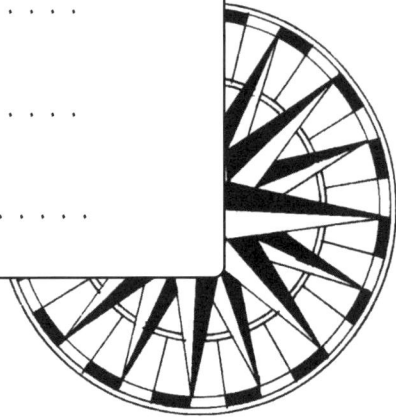

Passage Notes

HW

LW

TIME					

Date: . . . .

Crew: . . . .

. . . .

From: . . . .   Towards: . . . .

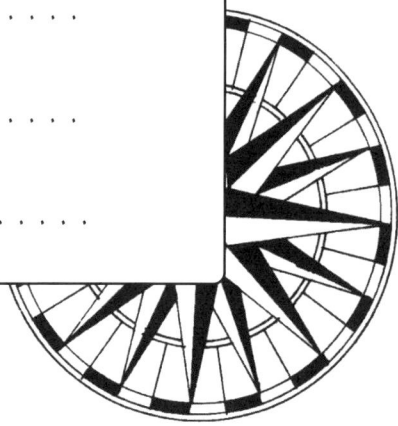

Passage Notes

HW

LW

TIME					

Date: . . . .

Crew: . . . .

. . . .

From: . . . .   Towards: . . . .

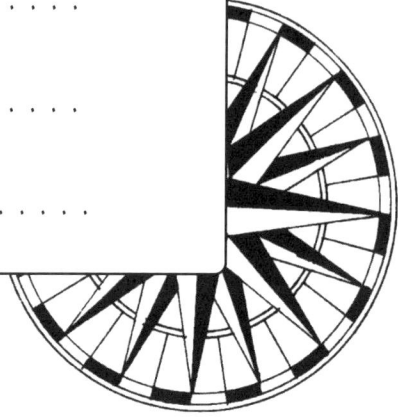

Passage Notes

HW

LW

TIME				

Date: . . . .

Crew: . . . .

. . . .

From: . . . .   Towards: . . . .

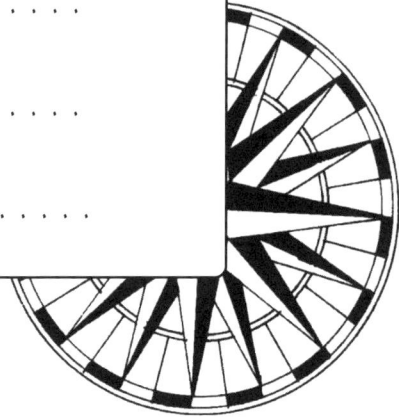

Passage Notes

HW

LW

TIME					

Date: . . . .

Crew: . . . .

. . . .

From: . . . .   Towards: . . . .

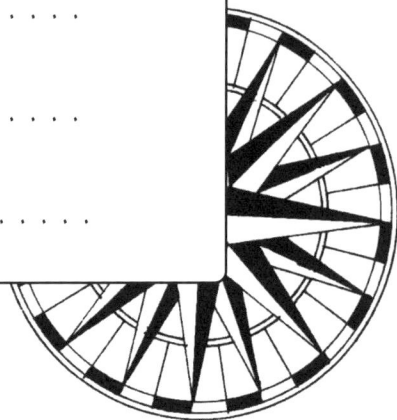

Passage Notes

HW

LW

TIME					

Date: . . . .

Crew: . . . .

. . . .

From: . . . .   Towards: . . . .

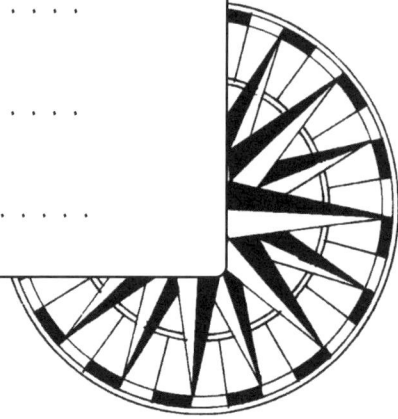

Passage Notes

HW

LW

TIME					

Date: . . . .

Crew: . . . .

. . . .

From: . . . .   Towards: . . . .

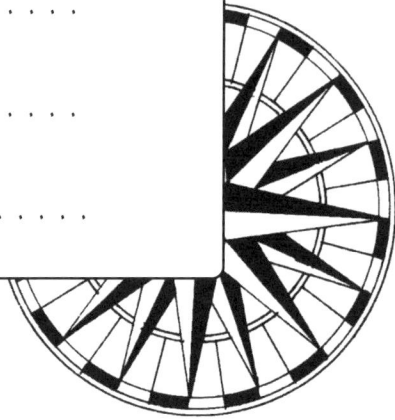

PASSAGE NOTES

HW

LW

TIME					

Date: . . . .

Crew: . . . .

. . . .

From: . . . .   Towards: . . . .

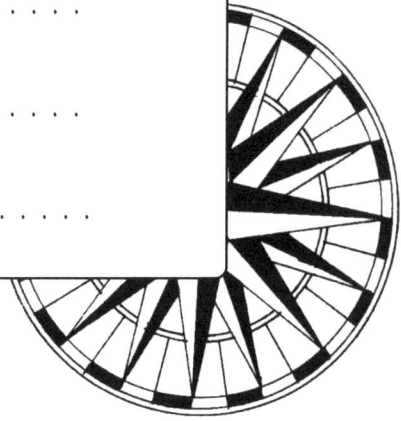

Passage Notes

HW

LW

TIME				

Date: . . . .

Crew: . . . .

. . . .

From: . . . .   Towards: . . . .

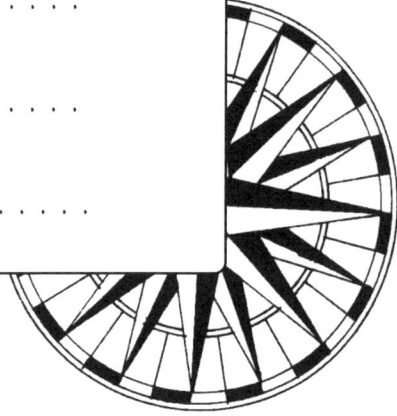

Passage Notes

HW

LW

TIME					

Date: . . . .

Crew: . . . .

. . . .

From: . . . .   Towards: . . . .

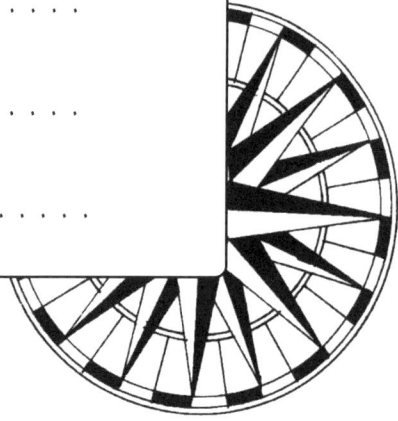

Passage Notes

HW

LW

TIME					

Date: ....

Crew: ....

....

From: .... Towards: ....

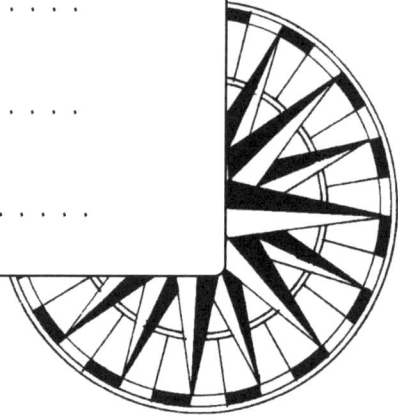

Passage Notes

HW

LW

TIME					

Date: . . . .

Crew: . . . .

. . . .

From: . . . . Towards: . . . .

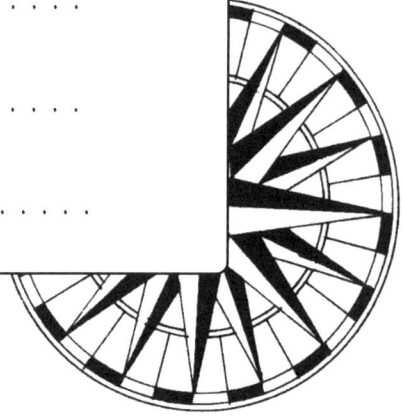

Passage Notes

HW

LW

TIME					

Date: . . . .

Crew: . . . .

. . . .

From: . . . .   Towards: . . . .

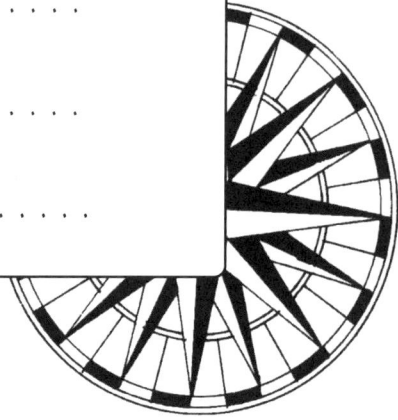

Passage Notes

HW

LW

TIME				

Date: . . . .

Crew: . . . .

. . . .

From: . . . .   Towards: . . . .

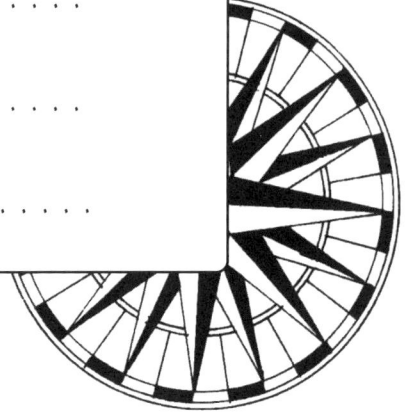

Passage Notes

HW

LW

TIME				

Date: . . . .

Crew: . . . .

. . . .

From: . . . .   Towards: . . . .

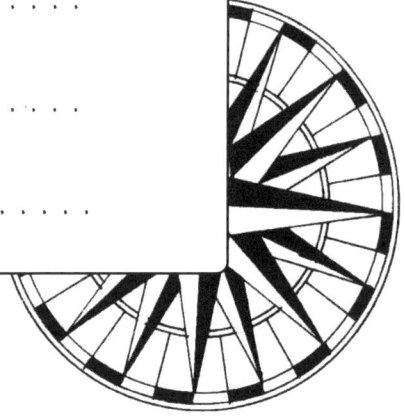

Passage Notes

HW

LW

TIME				

Date: . . . .

Crew: . . . .

. . . .

From: . . . .   Towards: . . . .

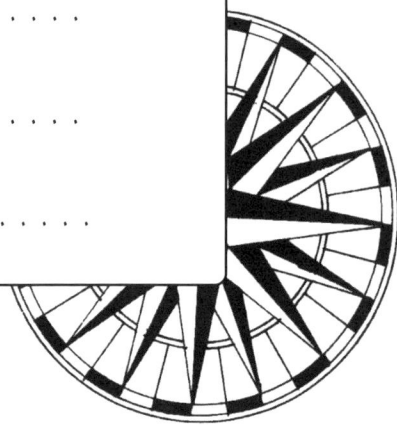

Passage Notes

HW

LW

TIME				

Date: . . . .

Crew: . . . .

. . . .

From: . . . .   Towards: . . . .

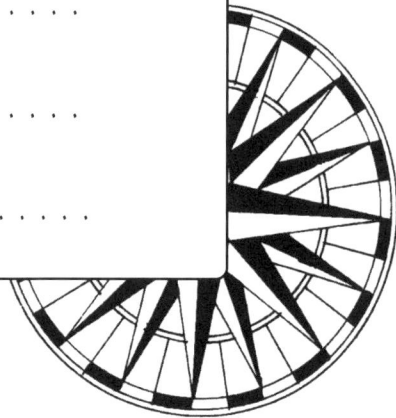

Passage Notes

HW

LW

TIME					

Date: . . . .

Crew: . . . .

. . . .

From: . . . .   Towards: . . . .

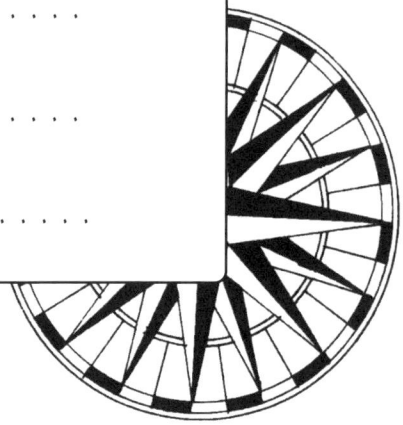

Passage Notes

HW

LW

TIME					

Date: . . . .

Crew: . . . .

. . . .

From: . . . .   Towards: . . . .

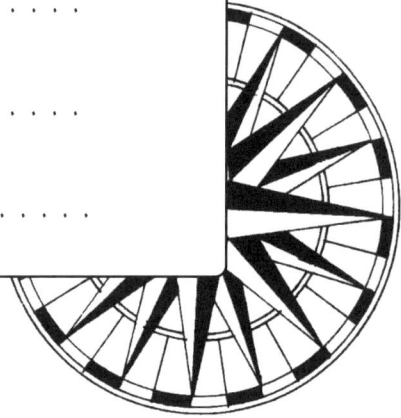

Passage Notes

HW

LW

TIME				

Date: . . . .

Crew: . . . .

. . . .

From: . . . .   Towards: . . . .

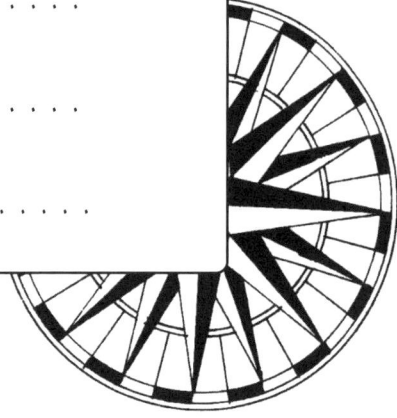

Passage Notes

HW

LW

TIME					

Date: . . . .

Crew: . . . .

. . . .

From: . . . .   Towards: . . . .

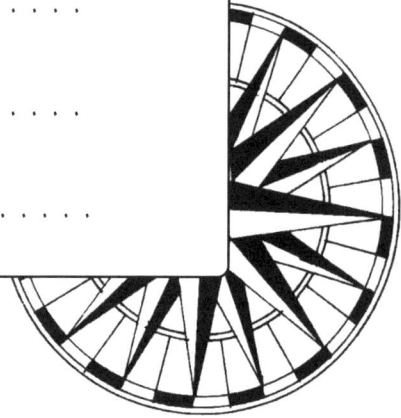

Passage Notes

HW

LW

TIME				

Date: . . . .

Crew: . . . .

. . . .

From: . . . .   Towards: . . . .

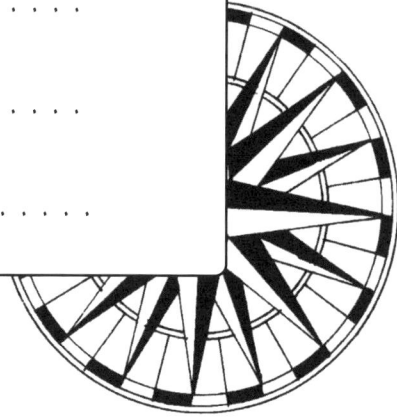

Passage Notes

HW

LW

TIME					

Date: . . . .

Crew: . . . .

. . . .

From: . . . .   Towards: . . . .

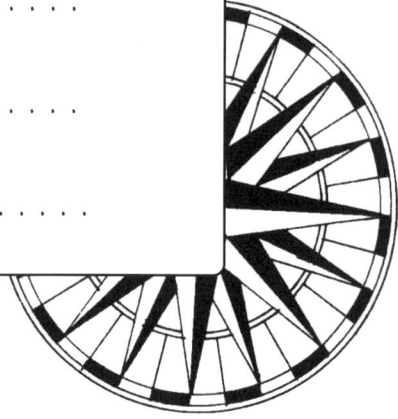

Passage Notes

HW

LW

TIME					

Date: . . . .

Crew: . . . .

. . . .

From: . . . .   Towards: . . . .

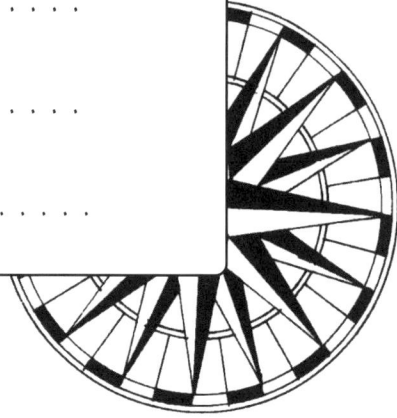

Passage Notes

HW

LW

TIME					

Date: . . . .

Crew: . . . .

. . . .

From: . . . .   Towards: . . . .

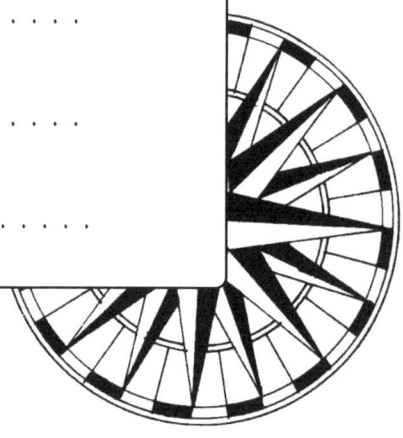

Passage Notes

HW

LW

TIME					

Date: . . . .

Crew: . . . .

. . . .

From: . . . .   Towards: . . . .

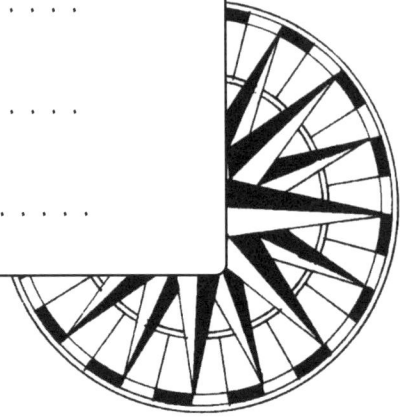

Passage Notes

HW

LW

TIME					

Date: . . . .

Crew: . . . .

. . . .

From: . . . .   Towards: . . . .

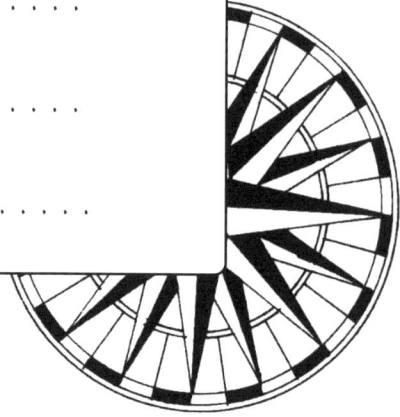

Passage Notes

HW

LW

TIME					

Date: . . . .

Crew: . . . .

. . . .

From: . . . .   Towards: . . . .

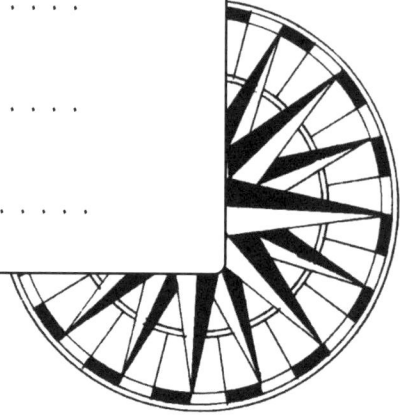

Passage Notes

HW

LW

TIME					

Date: . . . .

Crew: . . . .

. . . .

From: . . . .   Towards: . . . .

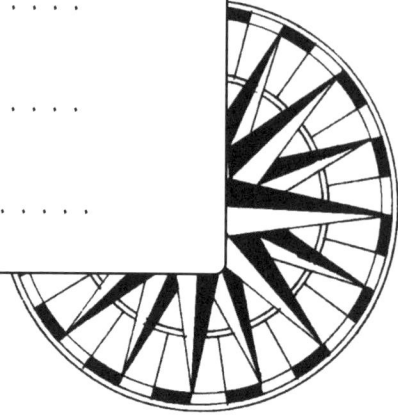

Passage Notes

HW

LW

TIME					

Date: . . . .

Crew: . . . .

. . . .

From: . . . .   Towards: . . . .

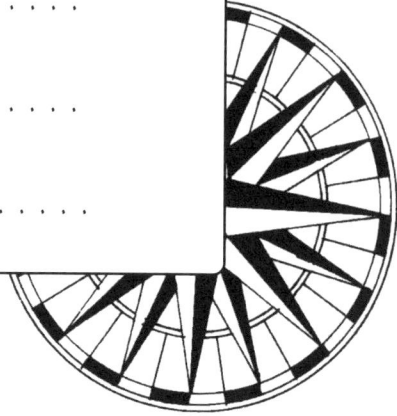

Passage Notes

HW

LW

TIME					

Date: . . . .

Crew: . . . .

. . . .

From: . . . .   Towards: . . . .

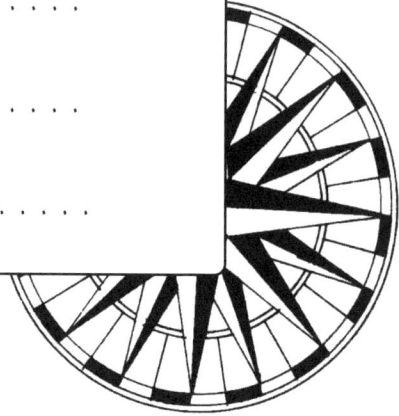

Passage Notes

HW

LW

TIME					

VISITORS

FRIEND-SHIP

Name	Address and telephone	Email/website:

Name	Address and telephone	Email/website:

Friendship knot

Name	Address and telephone	Email/website:

Name	Address and telephone	Email/website:

VISITORS

FRIEND-SHIP

Name	Address and telephone	Email/website:

Friendship knot

Name	Address and telephone	Email/website:

NOTES

lists....reminders....spares...notes

NOTES

lists...reminders...spares...notes

WEATHER FACTS

WIND SPEED CONVERSIONS

For an approximate conversion of miles per hour into knots, take off 15%. So a 20mph wind is 17 knots (force 5) To make it easy, remember that miles per hour is higher than knots - m for miles is also m for more.

For an approximate conversion of kilometres per hour into knots, halve it. A 10kph wind is 5 knots (force 2) but a 20kph wind is 11 knots (force 4).

Some European countries use metres per second - double the figure for an approximate conversion to knots.

BEAUFORT SCALE

0	Calm	(less than 1 knot)
1	Light airs	(1 – 3 knots)
2	Light breeze	(4 – 6 knots)
3	Gentle breeze	(7 – 10 knots)
4	Moderate breeze	(11 – 16 knots)
5	Fresh breeze	(17 – 21 knots)
6	Strong breeze	(22 – 27 knots)
7	Near gale	(28 – 33 knots)
8	Gale	(34 – 40 knots)
9	Severe gale	(41 – 47 knots)
10	Storm	(48 – 55 knots)
11	Violent storm	(56 – 63 knots)
12	Hurricane	(over 63 knots)

SPEED OF WEATHER SYSTEMS

Slowly	less than 15 knots
Steadily	15-25 knots
Rather quickly	25-35 knots
Rapidly	35-45 knots
Very rapidly	more than 45 knots

TIMING OF GALE WARNINGS

Imminent	within 6 hours
Soon	6 – 12 hours
Later	after 12 hours

VISIBILITY

Very poor	less than 1000m
Poor	1000m – 2 miles
Moderate	2 – 5 miles
Good	over 5 miles

SEA STATE

Smooth	less than 0.5m
Slight	0.5 – 1.25m
Moderate	1.25 – 2.5m
Rough	2.5 – 4m
Very rough	4 – 6m
High	6 – 9m
Very high	9 – 14m

FORECAST NOT GOOD, DEAR?

SUMMER BREEZE
MBYC